You know you're over 30 when...

WRITTEN BY
HERBERT I. KAVET

ILLUSTRATED BY
MARTIN RISKIN

COPYRIGHT 1988

IVORY TOWER
PUBLISHING COMPANY INCORPORATED

PUBLISHED SIMULTANEOUSLY IN CANADA BY MARKA CANADA ETOBICOKE, ONTARIO M9W 5Z6

DISTRIBUTED IN THE UNITED KINGDOM BY

WHYNOT PRODUCTIONS LTD. EAST SUSSEX TN21 OXL

DISTRIBUTED IN AUSTRALIA BY ABALNON PTY. LTD. CONCORD N.S.W. 2137

DISTRIBUTED IN NEW ZEALAND BY BLACKWOOD GAYLE DISTRIBUTORS AUCKLAND.

				6	7	8	9	10
11	12	13	14	15	16	16	18	
19	20	21	22	23	24	25		
26	27	28	29	30				

IVORY TOWER
PUBLISHING COMPANY, INC.
125 WALNUT STREET, WATERTOWN, MA 02172
TEL#: (617) 923-1111
FAX: (617)923-8839

You know you're over 30 when...

. . you don't believe all the things members of the opposite sex whisper in your ear. You don't get terribly embarrassed by them either.

You know you're over 30 when...

. . you can tell you've had enough to drink and nothing is
worth that hangover the next day.

You know you're over 30 when...

. . you finally realize that your mother isn't the greatest cook in the world. At least she remembers that you hate cauliflower.

You know you're over 30 when...

. . fine establishments actually solicit you to carry their credit cards.

You know you're over 30 when...

... you start taking a serious interest in investment and savings plans.

You know you're over 30 when...

. . you realize your father was right when he said it was as easy to fall in love with a rich person as a poor one.

You know you're over 30 when...

. . . you no longer apologize for your gay or weird friends.

You know you're over 30 when...

. . you start wearing underwear almost all of the time.

You know you're over 30 when...

. . you can buy a car without soliciting advice from your father.

You know you're over 30 when...

. . you can recognize and pronounce the names of at least 3 French wines.

You know you're over 30 when...

. . you fantasize about going into business for yourself.

You know you're over 30 when...

. . you've tried every known diet and no longer throw out your oversized clothes at the end of a successful one.

You
know you're
over 30
when...

.. you don't contemplate suicide at the end of a relationship.

You know you're over 30 when...

.. no matter how many sit ups and leg raises you do, you cannot recapture your 17-year-old figure.

You know you're over 30 when...

. . college-age people start calling you mister or ma'am.

You know you're over 30 when...

.. you leave parties early because the baby sitter has to be home by 11.

You know you're over 30 when...

.. you no longer get furniture from your relatives.

You know you're over 30 when...

. . you know exactly what you like, and what you like costs a fortune.

You know you're over 30

BINGLE HIGH SCHOOL REUNION

. . no one cares anymore about what you did in high school.

You know you're over 30 when...

. . being alone is better than being with someone you don't like.

You know you're over 30 when...

. . you no longer feel quite so "with it" and everyone who is "with it" seems to be 19.

You know you're over 30 when...

. . you worry about the long term effect of the sun on your skin but you still love a tan.

You know you're over 30 when...

ConservativE TowerS

. . you live in a place where noisy parties, littering, sex fiends, drug dealers and people crossing against the lights are all frowned upon.

You know you're over 30 when...

. . you start to trust banks (and they trust you).

You know you're over 30 when...

. . you no longer double date.

You know you're over 30 when...

. . you start having class reunions.

You know you're over 30 when...

. . they start treating you with real respect at your job.

You know you're over 30 when...

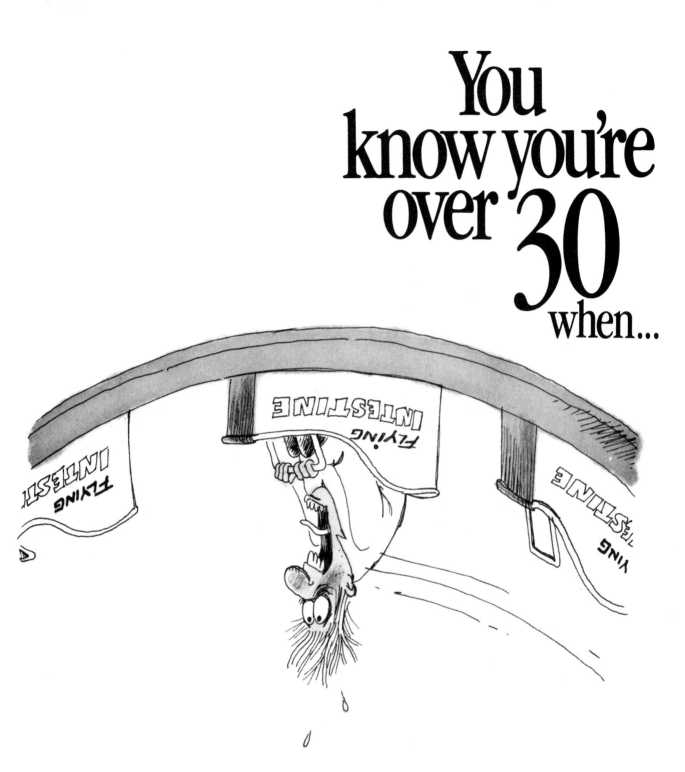

. . friends can't sucker you into really crazy activities.

You know you're over 30 when...

.. you no longer have to sedate yourself before speaking in front of groups.

You know you're over 30 when...

. . you find the first grey hairs!

You know you're over 30 when...

.. you're chosen to be the "designated driver."

You know you're over 30 when...

. . you can finally afford a vacation in a really exotic spot.

You know you're over 30 when...

. . you no longer party all night long.

You know you're over 30 when...

. . you receive daily mail promising enormous riches & fabulous prizes.

You know you're over 30 when...

. . you no longer have to lie on your resumé.

You know you're over 30 when

. . you're resigned to poverty for the rest of your life to accumulate a down payment on a condo you like.

You know you're over 30 when...

. . you finally hire someone to clean your place.

You know you're over 30 when...

. . your parents bug you to get married.

You know you're over 30 when...

. . your parents bug you to have children.

You know you're over 30 whe-

. . you've owned at least one car that's been totally paid for.

You know you're over 30 when...

. . you begin to realize you've slowed a bit since school.

You know you're over 30 when...

.. you're not afraid to complain about poor workmanship.

You know you're over 30 when...

. . you could eat a double fudge chocolate sundae and not get any pimples, but you'd have to exercise for 3 hours to work it off — so you skip it anyway.

You know you're over 30 when...

. . you know all the tricks for starting a car on a really cold day.

You know you're over 30 when...

. . your bookshelf is overflowing with "How To" and "Self Improvement" books but you've pretty well decided that you like yourself just the way you are.

IVORY TOWER PUBLISHING COMPANY INCORPORATED

These other fun books are available at many fine stores or by sending $3.50 ea. directly to the publisher.

2000-Do Diapers Give You Leprosy? A humorous look at what every parent should know about bringing up babies.

2008-Adult Connect the Dots. You played connect the dots as a child, but never like this!

2015-Games You Can Play With Your Pussy. And lots of other stuff cat owners should know.

2020-A Coloring Book for Pregnant Mothers To Be. Tender and funny, from being unable to see the scale to controlling you proud parents.

2026-Games You Can Play In Bed. A humorous compendium covering everything from Bedtime Bingo to Things To Do at 3:45 A.M.

2034-You Know You're Over Forty When... You Think "Grass" is something to cut and "Getting a little action" means your prune juice is working. A perfect 40th birthday gift.

2042-Cucumbers Are Better Than Men Because... They don't care if you shave your legs, and they never walk around your place when the shades are up. At last, ladies, revenge for all our male chauvinist books.

2059-Small Busted Women Have Big Hearts. Finally a book that boasts the benefits of being small busted in our society where bigger is better! A super way to bolster the ego of every slender woman.

2061-I'd Rather Be 40 Than Pregnant... Or worrying about getting into graduate school, or travelling with young children, or getting no respect at a ritzy store. Great moral support for women reaching the diaperless age.

2064-The Wedding Night-Facing Nuptual Terrors. For brides and grooms alike: What To Do If He Wants To Take Pictures; What To Do If She Won't Come Out Of The Bathroom; and many more hilariously funny situations newlyweds may encounter.

2067-It's Time To Retire When... Your boss is younger than you are, you stop to think and sometimes forget to start again, or you feel like the morning after and you swear you haven't been anywhere.

2068-Sex Manual For People Over 30. Includes great excuses for non-performance, rediscovering foreplay, and how to tell an orgasm from a heart attack.

2101-Peter Pecker's Guide To The Male Organ. A detailed analysis of the types of men who own Wee Wees, Members, Weenies, Dinks, Schlongs, No Nos, Tools, Wangs, and many others. Everyone is covered, from accountants to taxi drivers.

2102-You Know You're Over 50 When... You add "God willing" to the end of most of your statements and you don't care where your wife goes when she goes out, as long as you don't have to go with her. A great 50 year old birthday gift.

2103- Horny People. Find out who is horny(bosses and bearded men) and who is not(plumbers, skinny people and real estate agents) and why.

2109-The Get Well Book. Cheer up sick folks with this book that teaches them how to gain sympathy, what the doctor really means and how to cope with phones, kids, germs and critters that make you sick.

2121-More Dirty Crosswords. This latest edition of dirty crosswords will test your analytical powers even further as you struggle to improve your vocabulary.

2123-You Know You're Over 60 When... You're 60 when you start straddling two road lanes, you start looking forward to dull evenings at home, and you can't remember when prunes and figs weren't a regular part of your diet.

2126-After All These Years. An Anniversary Book. Gives all the pluses and problems of marriage from learning to sleep without pillows or blankets to having someone around who can find all the really itchy spots on your back.

2127-Your Golf Game Is In Big Trouble When... Your practice rounds are all in the bar and you've tried out 30 putters and none of them work and you play whole rounds without once hitting the fairway.

2129-Fun In The John. More fun than you ever dreamed possible. Crosswords, Bathroom Lists, Word Searches, Mystery Games, John Horoscopes, Connect The Dots, Mazes, and Much More.

2130-How To Tell If It Was Good. It was good if your partner can't stop repeating your name. It was bad if your partner can't remember your name. It was good if your partner wrote you poetry. It was bad if your partner wrote you a prescription.

2131-The Fart Book. Farts are divided into two groups. 1. Your farts. 2. Somebody else's fart. This book lists them all, the Little Girls Don't Fart Fart, The Dog Did It Fart, the S'cuse me Fart and many more.

2136-The Shit List. The list is quite extensive and describes the versatile use of this clever word. There is, for example, "chicken shit" and "give a shit" and "shoot the shit". A very funny book, No Shit.

2148-Dear Teacher...A hilarious collection of actual parents' notes to teachers. "Please excuse Joe from school yesterday. He had diarrhea through a hole in his shoe."

2153-Fart Part II. This sequel covers the dreaded "Thank God I'm Alone Fart", the insidious "SBD Fart" and the awe-inspiring "Sonic Boom Fart".

2166- You've Survived Catholic School When... You can enter a phone booth without feeling you should begin confessing and you don't shudder when someone hands you a ruler.

2168-You Know You're A Year Older When... You no longer eat all the dessert just because it's there and you can no longer easily sleep till noon.

2175-Asses. The complete directory of asses of all kinds from the Male Biker's Buns to the Oh Wow! Ass.

2177-You're Over the Hill When... No one cares anymore about what you did in high school, and you see your old cereal bowl in an antique shop.

2178-The Pregnant Father. The Pregnant Father's chief duty during delivery is to hold a little pan while his wife throws up into it...and much more!

2179-Irish Sex Manual. Great Irish lovers share their favorite positions. Learn why Irish women are better and what Irish men love about sex.

2180-Italian Sex Manual. Covers everything from picking up Italian men to great Italian sex games and why Italian men are better lovers.

2181-Jewish Sex Manual. Includes detailed information about what Jewish women love about sex, how to pick up Jewish men and great Jewish blind dates.

2183- 50 Is Fine If You Look 39... And you can eat a hot fudge sundae without worrying about breaking out. Plus many more!

2184- 60 Is Fine If You Look 39... And you can buy the car you want without worrying over whether it will hold ten kids, musical instruments and dogs. And more!

2186- 40 Is Fine If You Look 29... And you're still the same old tiger on the road, and they start to trust you at banks and you can still party with the best of them. For MEN.

2187- Big Busted Women Have More Fun... Big busted women somehow seem more motherly, get the most out of stretch fabric and always know where to look for a lost earring.

2188- Great Sex For Busy Couples... Explains how to find the time, the place and the desire when two careers keep the couple running.

2190- Teddy Bears Are Better Than Men Because... They don't hog the whole bed and they invariably understand when you have a headache.

2192-You Know You're Over 30 When... You start wearing underwear almost all of the time; you find the first grey hair and you no longer have to lie on your resume.

2193- The Bitch Book. The Bitch takes two spaces when she parks, is irritable every day of the month, and always goes through the express line at the supermarket.

2195- Beer Is Better Than Women Because... Beers don't want a lasting relationship, and beer doesn't expect an hour of foreplay before satisfying you.

2197- Tips for Successful Marriage... Tip 5: Every bride should carefully watch her figure and try to keep the groom out of it before the wedding, plus many humorous others.

2198- P.M.S. Book. What every woman experiences once a month. Includes the Irritability Syndrome, the Tender Boobs Syndrome and the Chocolate Syndrome.

2199- Men To Avoid... Certain types of men should be avoided at all costs. Among such types are the Mama's Boy, the Married Man and the Non-Performer.

2200- Shit Happens... It happens when the IRS asks for the receipts, your husband leaves you for an older woman, or you call suicide prevention and they put you on hold.

2202- Stressed Out... Being stressed out is trying to enjoy a cigarette in a non-smoking office, or having some kid park your brand new car.

2203- The Last Fart Book. This final sequel concludes with the Under The Cover Fart, the Waiting Room Fart, the Excuses Fart and many others.

2205- Is There Sex After 40? Normal 40-year olds do it once a week. Covers everything from sexy cardigans to tucking a vest into your underpants.

2206- Adult Party Games. Many original and some old favorite "permissively naughty" party games that will bring a party together and keep roaring through the night.

2207- Underwear. The complete directory of Underwear from the Old Fashioned Long Johns to The French Cut Briefs.

2208- Grandma's Birthday Is Special Because... Grandma lets you help blow out the candles and she gives YOU a present even though it's her birthday.

2209- Kissing For Fun. A riotous, richly illustrated collection of kisses from the dreaded Reception line kiss to the Hickey and the highly exotic French kiss.

2210- Is There Sex After Marriage? This great work covers everything from faking an orgasm to philandering to excuses for more or less sex. It even answers the age old question, Is There Sex After Pets?

2211- Boobs. Using the Standard Boob as a benchmark, this screamer examines the Pillow Boobs, Star Gazers, Spreaders, Ninnies, Disappearing Boobs, Oh Wow! Boobs and 40 others.

2212- Life With A Sports Junky. The Sports Junky spent part of his honeymoon in a grandstand, still ask his old coach for advice and thinks sex is O.K. as long as it is over by game time.

2213- Women Over 50 Are Better. They can tune out the worst snoring, have more womanly figures & won't make you sleep in the middle of a stuffed animal collection.

2214-Is There Sex After Divorce? All the funny situations when a middle aged person starts to date again, from not fooling around on the first date to finding a zit on your date ear.

2215-Over 65, The Golden Years? Great birthday and retirement gift. Describes "Bellies Are Beautiful", Early Bird Dinners", "Retirement, What Now?" and much more.

2216-Hanky Panky. Cartoons of the animal kingdom in their favorite amorous(and unmentionable) pastime. Brilliant full color drawings are riotously funny.

2217-Is There Sex After 50? Swapping your mate for two 25-year olds, finding places to put your cold feet, and telling grandchildren about when you were a hippy.

2218-Is There Sex After 60? Searching, in depth, cartoon report into the sexual behavior and horrible habits of the Don Juans of the Geriatric set. The Sewing Circle Seductress matches wits with the Casanovas of the Bingo Halls.

2219-Crosswords For Shitheads. For that person you feel is full of "it".

2220-Crosswords For Farters. A crossword puzzle book for people with gastrointestinal distress.

2221-Crosswords For Your Birthday. An irreverent crossword puzzle book for people who are terribly lonesome on their birthday.

2222-Crosswords For Bored Lovers. Designed to test you and your partner's sexual knowledge(or lack of it). Grab your lover, think sex, and dive in... to this collection of crosswords for those with a cloistered bawdy nature.

IVORY TOWER PUBLISHING CO., INC.   125 Walnut Street, Watertown, MA 02172   (617) 923-111